The Awakening of the Lions

My Rendition
of a
Patriotic Saint's Address

DONGMO DHYAN ANAND

outskirts press

My young sisters and brothers, I have ended my silence because circumstance demands it. "If the root of a tree begins decay, it spreads death to the branches" says a Nigerian proverb. You are the roots of our land. You will have the burden to bring either life or death to the national tree. And to bring life, you must have life in yourself. You might say that this manifesto is my attempt to invite you and show you how you can breathe life into our national tree. From which authority do you speak? I say I speak out of my own authority, but I echo in a different format the main wisdom of men of highest insight into the working of nature. I am not a mountain, but I humbly lean on mountains of the highest peaks. I have something to give, and I am starting to give it to you in the form of this appeal.

Appreciation or no appreciation, the time has come to galvanize my countrymen, especially its Youth. I want to send them rolling like a tsunami over Cameroon, bringing "morality," democracy, celebration and education. And this I am doing from the land of freedom where I find no impediment in my ability to work for my motherland. Young lions, pay heed to my words.

Be prudent, but be fearless. You will be kings. Remember, even lions hunt in herd. Join me and like-minded others to reestablish the balance of the shaking national triangle. Jump into the fire, if need be, to accomplish your work.

O Cameroon, beloved motherland. Remind us that your anthem exhorts us, children from the north to the south, from east to west to be love. O young lions, forget not that we are jealous of our freedom. You must not depend on any foreign help. Nations, like individuals, must help themselves. This is real patriotism.

Do not hate other races or nations; just understand that no individuals, no nation, can live detached from the community of others. Give and take is the way. If Cameroon wants to raise herself once more, it is absolutely necessary that she brings out her treasures and broadcast them to the world, and in return be ready to receive what others have to give. Expansion, openness, change is life. I thereby proclaimed a new form of nationalism. Not the abject nationalism that spreads hate and reclusion, but an expansionist nationalism.

Work in persistence for what matters. My heart continues to throb with love for you. This life comes and goes. Wealth, fame, enjoyment last but a few days. It is better to die laboring while preaching and living the highest ideals, than to die like worms. Stand up! Hold up! Advance!

Table of Contents

Prologue

The presidential elections of 2018 in Cameroon have revealed for this country the prospect of both a greater and a worse future. The challenge of the election results by the opposition party MRC (Movement Pour la Renaissance du Cameroon) has been carried through the Constitutional Court. This was an unprecedented event the broadcast of which has captivated the attention of about one million viewers both in the mainland and abroad. This successful viewership attests to a thirst among the citizenry of the country where freedom of speech, transparency, and the rule of fair law are implemented to achieve a stronger democratic system. The oratories of the different parties before the Constitutional Court captivate our country's potential as a future democratic nation.

On the other hand, the presidential election was conducted on the backdrop of threats by Boko Haram in the north, the secessionist war in the northwest and southwest, and the reemergence of the gruesome corpse of tribal ideologies. Terrorists of Mboko Haram have infiltrated our Septentrional region and have sown terror among our population to the extent that our country is officially at war in that region. In the southwest and the northwest province, secessionists of the auto-proclaimed "Ambazonia State" are fighting government troops; a fight that is making this economically important region barely governable. As if these two ills do not suffice, some politicians have exhumed the corpse of tribal identities to stir hate among the population.

In view of such a spectacle, I could not but be concerned, especially as our country will soon see the beginning of a new era. It is my conviction that the time has come for our country to reemerge as a continental cultural powerhouse, a regional economic and political lighthouse for the betterment of the children's lives. As our young nation prepares to celebrate its 2019 Youth Day, I henceforth write this manifesto as an appeal to the Youth of Cameroon.

FAITH AND STRENGTH

As soon as a man or a nation lose faith, despair comes, failure awaits, or death approaches. I indeed observed like many others, that the world's history is made by those who believed in themselves. Martin Luther King and Mahatma Gandhi are examples of men with strong belief in themselves, with strong desire to steer their countrymen to higher ground. Such men today would include Vladimir Putin, late US senators John McCain and "Ted" Kennedy.

Faith in ourselves, faith in God; therein lies the key to the hall of greatness. If we have faith in all the spirits, in all the gods, and we still have not faith in you, there is no salvation. Wise men of all times have asserted that nothing is impossible to the soul; "if you have a faith big like the sea….you can move a mountain," said Jesus. It is a heresy to say that you are not intelligent, not creative, unable to build a football stadium on par with college football stadiums in Europe. If indeed there is a sin in this case, the only sin is to deny yourselves all potentialities.

If you set reachable goals high, you are likely to come closer to whatever you think you can be. If you think of yourselves as strong, intelligent, creative, wise, it is more likely that you will build those qualities. Be free , hope for nothing from anyone. You have tried to get help from your government, or from foreign countries, but all their help has fallen short of lifting most of you out of misery or suffering. All the help that has come and is to come derives from yourselves. Why doubt your potential? Why say, "No, we cannot have vibrant democracy… it took hundreds of years for Europe to get there." Reject all these excuses, seize the opportunities that modern life offers, and make huge strides to a greater, better destiny. You are infinite, remember. Just close your eyes and see it for yourselves. See also the myriads of ideas that pass through the screen of your mind. Dig into them, sort them out. You can do more than you suspect. You are not destined to the lower levels of human evolution; you are not destined to the lower levels of socio-politico and cultural evolutions. Come up, young lions! Young indomitable lions! Shake off your delusions that you are but a sheep.

Never mind the struggles, the mistakes, the failures of the last thirty years or so. A monkey doesn't tell a lie, but he remains a monkey— never a man. So do not dwell on your failure. Hold the ideals of Cameroon with cleaner cities, with dynamic businesses and indus- tries, a Cameroon of political stability and alternate governance, a Cameroon where local cultures are examined, valued and preserved. Hold the ideals of a Cameroon so prosperous that her daughters and sons find joy and happiness in their homeland. Cherish those ideals a thousand times, and if you fail a thousand times, make one more attempt.

Be strong, my friends; that is my suggestion to you. You will be nearer to paradise through trade, industry, football as you study of scriptures. You will understand all your holy Scriptures better with your muscles, your biceps, your total attention to the tasks at hand. Wise men say that truth alone gives strength. And strength is the cure for disease. The fact is, life is strength and weakness is death. Strength is joy, resil- iency, prosperity. Weakness is constant misery, a sign of death.

To succeed in renewing your country, you must have a tremendous amount of perseverance; a huge will. You should be able to say, "I walk and the mountains crumble." "I can drink the ocean," states a persevering man. Have that sort of will, work steadily, and you will manifest your ideals.   We need strong, vigorous, believing young women and men, sincere to the backbone. A hundred of such in each province and our land will change to its core.

Death is better than a vegetative, ignorant life. Die on the battlefield rather than live a life of defeat. Come and do something heroic! Reject the literal interpretation of "Happy are the poor, for they will inherit the Kingdom of God."   Being full of holy thoughts, words and deeds, should not prevent you from entering into the field of action in a way that benefits the world. Can anything be done unless one exerts himself to his utmost? Know that the God of wealth resorts to men of action--to the lion-hearted man. No need to look behind. Move forward, Look forward! Infinite energy, infinite patience, infinite devotion have to be assembled for great things to be achieved. The road is challenging. But be not in despair; arise, awake and find the ideal.

Let people say whatever they like. Stick to your own convictions. Some say to you, "Have faith in this fellow or that fellow. But I say to you: Have faith in yourself first. I've heard from higher authorities that even the poison of the snake is powerless if one can firmly deny it. Remember Nelson Mandela's fearlessness and fierceness in facing the apartheid regime; remember his ideal, the ideal of a free south Africa "This is an idea for which I am prepared to die," he said. There is a lesson for life- face the terrible, face it boldly.

Stand up and fight! Not one step back, that is the idea. Fight it out, whatever comes. Let the star descend upon us. Have you gained anything by becoming a coward? America, the land of the free, is great because a few men stood against the kingdom of Europe, and unleashed a set of bold actions and ideas that continue to sustain the country's position as a lighthouse. By taking a step backward , you do not avoid misfortune. You have prayed for decades; you have poured oil on the skulls or implored the spirits; Has your misery ceased? So what is the point of being timid, fearful? It does not benefit you to be a slave. Arise! Wake up! Get up and fight for better city planning, better schools, better roads, more parks and attractions… Fight for your dignity and for the dignity of the land where you happened to be born.

The Power of Self Restraint

Pick up an idea and make of it the main focus of your thinking, of your dream. Let the brain, nerves and every part of you, soak in that idea and just leave other ideals alone. For that you must go deeper into yourself. Reputable authorities have stated that this deepening and concentration are the ways to success.

Concentration is an intense assimilation. The more concentrated you are, the more knowledge you acquire. Look at your goalkeeper; the more concentrated he is, the more ball kicks he tends to catch. The cook with concentration will cook a better meal. In making money, in worshipping, in whatever you do, the stronger the power of concentration, the better that thing will be done.

Wise men of the highest kind contend that the knowledge of work can only be gained by concentration of the powers of the mind. Someone said that the world is ready to offer its secret if we only know how to give it the necessary blow. And that strength and the force of that blow comes through concentration.

We think of ourselves as free. Can we for one moment control our body, our mind, or can we hold it on a subject? A mind, let loose or uncontrolled, will drag us down, enslave us, and even kill us. Likewise, a mind controlled and guided will save us. It is indeed the power of concentration and self-restraint that differentiates men and animals, the lowest and the highest creatures.

Good and evil thoughts are each a potent power which fill our surroundings. They remain in forms of thought until translated into action. You know there is latent force in arms until you strike a blow. We are heirs of good and evil thoughts. If we make ourselves pure and the instrument of good thoughts, these will enter us. A good person cannot be receptive of evil thoughts.

You have probably noticed there are men and women who seem to have from birth a mission to accomplish in the world. When they speak, their word is direct, poignant. They seem unconcerned by the rhetoric, the style, the language; for these are of secondary importance. What is important is whether or not you have something to give. It is a question of giving and taking, and not listening. Do you have anything to give? – If you have, then give.

Whatever you do, devote your entire mind and heart to it. No need to hide in a church, in a mountain, or in your house. No need to refrain from living, from dancing, from being involved in the life if your villages, cities, departments and provinces. If your (body and) mind is not under control, it is no use living in a monastery or in a church. The same mind will bring troubles there.

It is your mental attitude which makes the world what it is for us. Our thoughts make things beautiful or they make them ugly. In that sense our world is the reflection of our mind. Strive then to see things with the proper light.

ONE

You Are The Maker

Be good. Make it a choice to be so, not because of Jesus, Mohammed or whoever you believe to be good. Do it for yourself.

You are responsible for what you are today. Make no mistake about it, your experiences, your choices and your genetics have led you to what you are today. So whatever you want to be in the future can be produced by your present actions. So learn the art to act.

You have heard that a man is a man as long as he strives to rise above his internal and external nature. Each of you has to work on his own salvation; the same for nations. It is one thing to criticize the institution of our country, to denounce corruption, to point to unpassable streets and poor road infrastructure. But remember, you will be a real humanitarian, an extraordinary citizen if you help your fellow countrymen overcome their limitations within the system in which they live. If individuals are raised, the nations and their institutions are bound to rise.

A wise lady once said, "the world is governed from inside out." Hence you have to grow from inside out. You are well aware of human tendency to lay blame of life's problems upon his fellow humans, God or upon fate. Stay clear of such a habit. We reap what we sow. You are the maker of your fate. Is it the fault of the wind if the vessels with undeployed sails cannot catch it? So young lions, say :"My condition is that of my own doing, as such it will be undone by me." No one else will remove you from hell. Therefore stand up and be bold when the circumstances demand it.

Make your own future. Let the dead past bury its dead. An infinite future is ahead of you. And keep in mind that each word, thought and action bring about a future for you. Keep in mind that bad thoughts and bad work will insidiously grow like a cancer.

It is unfortunate that many of you want to go through life without an ideal at all. If it is indeed true that a man with an ideal makes one thousand mistakes; the man without ideals would make fifty times more mistakes. Therefore it is better to have an ideal. Do not waste your time complaining and quarreling. It won't help you makes things better. Grumble at little things and you will grumble at everything; you will live a miserable life, and you may end up a failure. But do your duty, and you will see greater duty fall under your responsibility.

Humans of deep insight into life affirm that every thought, after a certain time goes into seed form and lives in our body as potential. Later it emerges and bears its fruits. These results condition our lives. This is how you mold your own life.

Integrity, patience and perseverance are important ingredients for success, but love is above all. By love, understand the recognition that your neighbor, your classmate, countrymen…put simply, they are all made in the image of God. This means: the others, including you, is a manifestation of God. Therefore you should approach her or him cautiously. Never forget that fact in your dealings with others.

Life appears to be a continuing expansion, while contraction appears to be death. For a person, seeking only his personal comfort and leading a lazy life, a Saint once said there is no room for such a human even in hell. Use your reason, and if it proves to be consistent with the truth of the great men you heard about, then you shall believe them.

Do not deny your own experience. Believe Jesus, Mahomet, Buddha and any great men of the past. Believe these men when you see similar prophets or men of great wisdom around you. Remember, these men were not peculiar men, but only illustrative of certain principles or a certain quality. That is why we respect and bow to them.

Try to get it right once. Why become wise through failure? Time is indeed infinite. Look at the rock—it never steals, yet it is always a rock. Look at the monkey, he never tells a lie, but he remains a monkey all the time. Do something! It is better to do something, even if you get it wrong; it is better than doing nothing. Apply yourself to doing good. Think holy thoughts continuously. That is a way to suppress the lower impressions. Don't think yourself as hopeless because you represent a character, an assemblage of habits, which can be replaced by new and better ones: "Character is repeated; habits and repeated habits alone can reform character."

You can overcome difficulties by constant practice. Nothing can happen to you unless you avail yourself to action; unless you make yourself impressionable, susceptible. An Asian proverb says: "It is the coward and the fool who says 'This is fate'." Strong men, young men stand up and affirm "I will create my own fate." A Greek philosopher once said that if you want to gauge the character of a man, look not at his great performances. Any fool may become a hero at one time or another. Watch a man carrying out his most common actions; those are really indicators of his real character. Great occasions can rouse even the lowest human being to some kind of greatness; but only to the great man, whose character is always great, the same wherever he is.

Good thoughts that you send to the world, without thinking of any return, is reported to be stored up in the skies. There it will break up one link in the chain of evils and make you purer. Project hatred, jealousy, and selfishness and it will rebound on you multiple-fold. No powers are reported to avert them. Remember this. That will prevent you from doing wicked things.

In whatsoever struggles inside and outside you, there lies consciousness. Just try to kill a cockroach, it will resist to save its life. Your freedom, the expansion of your life may be limited by abject poverty, repression, oppression. What would you naturally do? Resist. Resist so that your life, your consciousness reaches its peak. How to resist? Do this either by work, worship or philosophy. Do it by one, more or all of these and be free. That is religion. A religion indistinct from your daily life. Doctrines, dogmas, rituals, temples are of secondary importance.

Embody, O Lions the spirit of tolerance. What food is good for you, may be indigestible for another. We have been put into a jack's-fit-all sized box. The uneducated, the uncultured, unthinking men and women! Think for yourselves! Exercise your mind! What right do you have to say this person is wrong? It may be wrong to you; that is to say if you adopt his method, you will fail. All of you will be degraded; but that does not mean he will be degraded. Your fathers ' ways have been looked upon with contempt; the invaders have imposed democratic ways and many other policies. What good have all those foreign influences done for you? You have to learn to value your own ways, yet be open to others. You have already embraced the foreigners' way. Don't revert back. Use it, but enrich it with your own ways so as to make your life richer, happier, and more fulfilling.

TWO

Education and Society

Education, real education should enable you to stand on your own two legs. So far our education has not equipped us to endure the struggles of life. It does not bring out strength of character, a spirit of philanthropy, or the courage of a lion. Where is the courage to say "no" when your compatriots are shot in the legs during a peaceful protest? Where is your courage in face of rampant corruption, the abject incompetence of your elected officials? And you claimed to be educated?

Is learning a factual body of knowledge what you call education? Being a medical doctor is to have learned enough data about the human body, is it not? Being a political scientist is to engage in forays into the theories and practice of politics, is it not? This body of learning can give you some insight into one department of life, but you will agree that you are still ignorant in many other areas, including life itself. All we tend to do is to intellectualize everything. We use our left brain faculty a lot, forgetting that our right brain exists. Is the collection and manipulation of data what you called education? The African immigrants are among the highest learned in the US. Has that body of learning translated into creativity in political, social and economic spheres? We have plenty of Ph.Ds in Cameroon? Has that diplo-might" brought the boon we would have expected?

Education should not be reduced to adding all your life to your brain's information which once it is activated, forms a myriad of combinations that we retrieve when there is a need. I subscribe to the notion that education is about assimilation of ideals that prepare one for survival, in the struggle of life, and how to live in harmony with our surroundings. If you assimilate just three ideals and make them your life and character, you have more education than any graduate of any so-called elite schools who have focused on using his intellect in a foray into a one body of knowledge. Note that the history of the world is not made by learned men, but by educated men. If you can be both educated and learned, then the world will benefit immensely.

A great service to be done for our Youth is to give them education. Give them ideas, ideals and the rest will follow. If poverty prevents our Youth from getting educated, education must be given to them. We want that education which enhances character, strengthens the mind, and expands the intellect so that you can stand on your own two feet. We should not copy-and-paste Western education. I rather see us going wrong by our own free will and intelligence than be seen as automatons, or as intellectual parrots. What we want is Western science, Eastern philosophy--all blended with African wisdom and faith in ourselves.

Our education must repose on a strong life-building course by teachers well versed in African history and wisdom, Western sciences and Eastern philosophies. Like their counterpart in health professions, teachers should be exemplars of sound ethics and the object of public respect– for the welfare and the future of the country depend on them. Look at our schools and universities, how many original men and women have they molded? I mean men and women willing to sacrifice for the welfare and the well-being of our nation? How many Roger Millas , Bernard Djongas, or Maurice Kamtos? Traveling the cities of America, I have met countless such men and women, not very learned, but whose work ethics and sense of civism speak volumes about the love for protecting and improving the ways of life of their nation. That's what we are lacking.

Young lions, you have the potential to create hundreds of original men. Be ready to work, worship and philosophize for the sake of improving your countrymen and your country's condition; then you will be happier and our nation will recognize you. Don't be afraid to atone for the common good if circumstance demands it. Be a humanist like Jon Snow of the Game of Thrones. "He who saves his life will lose it, and he who gives his life for others will be saved," said one Scripture. And the statement is Truth in the sense that by working for others , motivated by love, one expands one's life. Truth does not pay homage to society; rather society has to pay homage to truth or perish. That society is the greatest where the highest truths become practical. Look at America, the land of the free. America has understood that God respects the freedom of man, so the American constitution guarantees individual freedom to a great extent. This practical implementation of the Freedom-Truth, in my view, accounts for the tremendous creativity that set this nation apart. Therefore, young Lions, rise to the Truth of Goodness, Freedom, Sacrifice.

Comfort and luxury should not be the ideals. Not that they contain something inherently wrong; they are mere conveniences that pale in comparison to the boon that higher ideals can bring. If your ideal is solely matter, matter shall you be: Make of Freedom, Courage, Peace, Goodness and Progress your ideals. They are spirit-like ideals, and as such they have a prolonged lifespan. Take up these ideals, devote yourselves to them, struggle with them with patience and soon you will see the shining light at the end of the tunnel.

Do not mind others criticisms and attempts to destroy you, for they are more ignorant than you. Wickedness is ignorance, weakness. Let me tell you that you are capable of higher achievement. It is in your nature- For the world is indeed governed from inside out. Be open to adapt. No reform is needed in your land. Let the scholars keep their fancy words and ideas. Nothing is too difficult in our land to reform. Remain flexible and adaptable. Those who adjust themselves best live. The word around you is change. Adapt, change, evolve!

On one side the Youth is thinking: "if we only adopt Western ideas, Western language, Western food, Western dress and Western manners, we shall be as strong and powerful as Western nations." On the other side the old African griot says: "Does the ass in lion's clothes become a lion?" Don't be short-sighted! By imitation, other's ideas never become one's own. Nothing is your own unless earned. First, try to find ideals within your own soul, your national soul. You have earned these ideas over time; they are valid as long as you give them a new rendition to fit the times. Thereafter, learn from others. Gain what you can and give it a new rendition that fits your environment, your experience, your personality. See how you are struggling to understand democracy. For you, the president is the chief who needs your constant praise, who must stay in office for life, to whom you owe your daily life… These are the ways you have seen your traditional chiefs. But wake up! Enter into modernity! You have adopted the Western democracy, copy it well. If not, give it a new facelift to make the instrument, the vehicle for the highest ideals of Freedom, Progress in your land. Don't clothe Western democracy with the attire of the antique past and its lowest level of evolution. Rather, clothe it with the best attributes of our ancient system of governance: For example, the checks- and -balances provided by the nine notables in the traditional polities of the North and the West.

In our ancestral days, we Africans have challenged the world: not by lineage, not by individual wealth alone, but wisely dissolving our individuality into the group individuality. If not, no merriment, continence and balanced minds can be achieved. And for hundreds of thousands of years, this has been our way. Races in Asia and in other parts of the world have come to the same realization; they have built upon it

and taken up higher challenges. Unfortunately, we have remained stuck
at the first riddle and its solutions. And subsequent contacts with
foreign forces have made us amnesiacs. Now we are trying to solve
with foreign tools the riddle we have solved ages ago. Let me make
clear, we have already solved the challenge of achieving individual happiness, merriment and balance of mind. And our solution: renunciation
of members individuality so as to allow the group to prosper.

THREE

Serve Your Countrymen. Serve Your Country

Our duty to our country is to help our fellow countrymen and to do good to the country. Remember, by doing good to your country, you really help yourselves, your parents, your family, your friends.

Don't take too much pride in the fact that you donate books to the local schools or supplies to the local medical center. But be grateful that unequipped schools and clinics are there so that your donations are opportunities to help yourselves. Our land remains in great need of hospitals, clinics, schools, skill training centers, clean water, and safe road infrastructure just to name a few. These are opportunities in which you should be involved; these are opportunities for you to help yourselves. Do not say: "I do not have anything to give." Because you do. Give what you can. And remember the words of wisdom: "It is more blessed to give than to receive," Act 20:35.

Doing good, being involved in your country's affairs is a great work. How can you live in a house and pay no attention to its crumbling walls, its falling roof, to the snakes roaming in your backyard? Take full ownership of your property! Your country is your land, it is yours to manage. You may choose to hire someone to manage your affairs; but if the hire fails to make your land prosperous, what would you do? The appropriate actions would be to replace him or her. You will leave behind your various connections to him or her and do what is right for your affairs to prosper. You cannot fathom that the hire would trick you to keep his job. You cannot imagine him threatening and hurting other workers and some of your relatives who protest his handling of your affairs. Wouldn't that be hysterical? What would you do then? I suspect you will demand and force his departure using all legal means. And if the legal means are biased against you, sacrifice in non-violent manners. Share your plight with your workers, relatives, neighbors and friends, and walk with them in the offices, in the hallways and sit there, resolutely disciplined till justice is rendered. And if attempts are made on your life, defend your life to the utmost.

Your country is your property. Take full ownership of it. Don't be passive. Don't be lazy. Do not allow oppression, repression, incompetence to be the way of your land. Do not turn blind eyes to these vices or evil deeds, because their subsequent effects have not yet reached your door. Don't be complicit. Stop evils practiced through covert and overt actions.   There is no neutrality. In refusing to act overtly or covertly, you partake of that evil. You have the damned duty to choose. Approach reality with neutrality; I know it is not easy, but strive to see and listen with neutral eyes and ears so as to have a sound appreciation; then act. Refusing to act is also an action. I subscribe to the sound theory that the action one has done cannot be destroyed till its residual effects have been manifested or destroyed by a force greater in nature. Do not support the inappropriate actions! Do not resort to intellectual gymnastics to justify crimes, repressions, oppression, killings, persistent unemployment, corruptions, embezzlement of public resources. Your elders have justified these vices for so long. And now they are reaping falling infrastructures, nontransparent elections, dirty cities, power shortages and incompetent management. These are some of the fruits of many years of passivity, of turning blind eyes. The future is in your hands. Do good to your countrymen, do good to your country. And no force can prevent these actions from bearing good fruits.

Right now our land abounds in acts of injustice, nepotism, tribalism, and mismanagement, just to name a few. Go out into the injustice and struggle to lessen it or die in the attempt. Remember, dying mostly into ourselves to allow our group to prosper, is the way we Africans have ages ago solved the challenge of individual versus group prosperity. So let us go back to the source. The first step to success in this endeavor entails forgetting. Forget your ideologies—socialism, capitalism, and other ism; forget your identification to your tribe- Bamiliekes, Fangs, Peuls… Forget your religious identification—theist, atheist, agnostic, Christian, Muslim, animists. What is the use of all these ideas and their subtle doctrines? Do good deeds to your countrymen and your land undistinctive of their identification. Adzaba, Moustapha, Djoulde, Domyou, Bona, Bedzigui, Beyala, Amoute, Moudi, Bivina,.. these are just names. What should matter to you is that they are countrymen first. Don't care too much about where they happened to be born. Do good to them and be good to the land to which we all belong. Such an attitude will take us far.

Work not for money or fame. These are lesser motives. Find a greater motive. Work to make your country famous, to make your country richer. Be more ambitious! Your nations should be your ambition, not only advancing your small person. O young lions, devote yourself to that ambition and out of it will come a power to work in such a manner that you will transform yourself. As such you will transform your country. If you want prosperity, bring every day a little joy and peace into the heart of your countrymen. Your leaders are frustrating you because their actions do not bring a little more celebration into your life, a little more freedom to propose and innovate, a little more money to upset the rising costs of living. You do not need fancy economic or social theories to understand the basic yearnings of human life. So, choose as your leaders only those who can bring and sustain peace, celebration, and decent income. If she or he has failed to bring these into your life, or is no more able to do so, gently thank this individual for the service and find someone else. No one is indispensable.

For ages, sacrifice has been and remains the way to go. The bravest among you will have to atone for the welfare of all. Such men are necessary by the hundreds in every corner of our land. Let us not dissipate our energy in unnecessary drinking and futile meetings. Advance brave lions! Advance, brave women and men, to set those who are in unjustified captivity, to lessen the burden of misery, to illuminate the abyss of darkness among ignorant brothers and sisters. Bring back multiple-fold the glory of the seventies and the eighties. For our place is among the stars of the continent and the known of the world.

One way to get your potential manifested is by helping your countrymen to discover or to manifest their own potential. Even though inequality is noticeable in Nature, wise men say there is still equal chance for all—yet greater for some and less for others. So the weaker should be given more chance than the strong.

To you, fellow countrymen of the diaspora, here is my appeal to you: Great help must be given to our sisters and brothers living back home, where institutions are not keen to promote greater freedom of expression, individual rights, and greater survival rates for most people. You have at your disposal legal resources, and institutional tools that you can leverage to bring an end to oppressive and repressive governments. Whosoever clings to power to hold our countrymen in bondage is neither stronger nor fiercer than was the apartheid regime in South Africa. Victory is a likely possibility. But it is up to you. Not a single foreigner will do it for you. Some might even oppose, depending on the size of their interests in our land. But I've noted that they often yield in an attempt to control the transition when the indigenous have built a critical mass and are on the verge of achieving victory over the stubborn leaders. No need to blame them, it is natural for one to protect his investment. What is needed from you is to help build a critical mass, and that requires persistent and consistent efforts in partnership with our countrymen in the mainland.

Prayers can be vain. "If the sacrifice of a lamb can send a man to the gate of heaven, what about the sacrifice of a man?" asked a Saint. Be Abraham and say: "Sacrifice me." Death is certain. Thus it is better to die for a good cause. I see death as a gradual process with love as its peak as well as its twilight-like metamorphosis into life. Some will die at 50 or 60—others at 80, 90 or even 100 percent. It does not matter. Die first of your own volition. This world is not for cowards, sitting behind media of various kinds, belitting some, blessing others, while doing nothing concrete when the circumstance demands it. This world is not for those who just talk but cannot walk when the circumstance demands it. Lions in Yaounde, Douala and all major cities of the land, Lions in Europe, America, Africa and Asia. Be ready to stand wisely in the whirl and in the madness of actions when the circumstances demand, and discover your soul as a nation, as a person.

We need ten thousand women and men, fired with the zeal of freedom, fortified with faith in themselves, and nerved with lions' courage. They will also be fueled by empathy for the oppressed and the repressed or by love for their land. They will march non-violently, and brave the plastic baton rounds and/or the real bullets. They will preach in the main squares of each capital the gospel of justice, of transparency, of better governance, and that of social uplifting.

Military and uniformed personnel, You vowed to devote yourselves to the defense of the land and its highest ideals, and to the protection of your countrymen. You embody its utmost spirit of sacrifice I have called for in your Youth. And you deserve our respect and our praise for that. But where is your martial spirit when you shoot peaceful and unarmed civilians in the legs? Martial spirit, I understand as one's ability to know how to serve and obey, and how to practice self-restraint. The martial spirit is not self–affirmation, but devotion to others, sacrifice to a cause higher than oneself. In this instance, this cause is the country. And who makes the country? Its people – the president is just the people's mouthpiece and the chief executive officer of the land. Therefore, it is emphatically your duty, the duty of the military and uniformed personnel to protect the people. You are the guarantor of the stability of our institutions, as long as they bring joy, a smile, celebration, fulfillment to the people you protect. If these institutions objectively do not fulfill their duties , due to the egocentrism or the narcissism of some elected officials, you can legitimately protect the people in their peaceful demands and their protests against such leaders. For your devotion is to the nation, to the people, then to the elected representative. Without being a military expert, I suspect that military strategy demands that one protects its most valuable assets. In a wartime situation, who do you need the most? The people will cheer for you, they will bake bread, fries beignets, make fufu, grilled corn and plantain for you to eat; its women are ready to hit the factory to supply you with weapons, foods and all other necessities. Would a president or an elected representative do that for you? I do not mean to minimize the role of elected representatives; all I am trying to indicate is that you should only show an unrelenting allegiance to the elected representatives that best meet the people's needs. Refrain from taking over as we have seen in many countries, but facilitate the democratic game to continue smoothly for the benefit of your children, wife, parents, friends—all those who are among the people you have vowed to protect.

Young brothers, sisters: Tell your parents or friends who are men and women in uniform: Your duty is to protect the people; and extend that protection to those who disagree peacefully with the leaders of the country. Encourage them this way: Dad, Mom, Uncle, Brother, Sister, please promise me to serve the people and protect the people in the face of unjust law or unjust administrative policies which take away the freedom and undermine the expression of the will of the people.

Young lions, nature has set me on this foreign land; and I made it my land. But can the mother and the child be disconnected? Your land is my mother. A child is never disconnected from his mother. I have been physically disconnected from you, but the spiritual connection is never disconnected. I call upon you to show sympathy to your countrymen, to struggle for the poor, the repressed, the oppressed. I exhort you to open all the doors and windows of your houses and cars to look at the people sunk in misery in the slums of Nlongkak. Noticed the long lines at the Immigration Police Office. Look at the condition of the highly traveled Yaounde-Douala. Look at the dusty, dirty streets of Yaounde, and the anarchic construction. Note the excessive numbers who are daily controlled by alcohol and its correlation to the increased incidence of cardiovascular accidents. Read the posts on social media, and see how many are calling for our nations to be split. Note all these observations, young lions, and vow that you will devote yourself to do a little every day for this self-destructing nation and its 26 million people.

Few men—In fact, six men of faith and pure character have made the history of the world. Hence it is my understanding that three ingredients are sufficient to unleash success: compassion, a brain to conceive, and hands to work. The last two ingredients are self-explanatory and easy to understand; only the first merits some precision. Through compassion, you are invited to assess your feelings for your nation. Do you feel love, hatred, jealousy or indifference to your countrymen or your country? It is not uncommon to see great work undermined by the jealousy, the hatred and the anger we pour out there in the universe. Be pure, love your countrymen, and your strength will multiply.

FOUR

Ethics and Religion

Religion can be considered as a social program to humanize the mentality, to raise the brute onto a man, then to a God. One difference between God and devils lies in unselfishness and selfishness. In scriptures, the devil is presented as knowing as much as God, but he lacks holiness, love. Hence, excess of power and knowledge, without love, makes human beings devils.

Virtue entails that which improves us, while vice is that which contributes to our degeneration. Of these three qualities: brutality, humanity, and godliness; what brings out our divinity is virtue, and what increases our brutality (animality) is vice. The choice is yours to make. You have heard 'God is within you." You have been told "you are created in the image of God." There is tremendous truth to it. Therefore if you cannot worship with your countrymen the manifested God, how dare you worship the unmanifested God? "Not he that cries, "Lord, Lord," but he that doeth the will of the Father." Here is the essence of religion. Practice good and do good. By good, I mean what is right. By what is right, I understand what is appropriate for the time and the circumstance.

I have seen religions and cults flourish in your midst. So you should be happier, more involved and invested in your countrymen's well-being. True religion brings peace, happiness, and humanity. Be really religious then! A successful religion yields economic benefits. Therefore, be more religious in the true sense; as a corollary, you will be more industrious and more sensitive to the welfare of your countrymen.

Be moral, be courageous. Don't bother with religious theories. Courageous men don't sin. By morality, understand "that which creates less harm and bring peace and happiness to others." By immorality, understand: that which mostly brings happiness and joy to one only, and less to others. So adopt this understanding as your code of ethics and transform your country.

Cameroon: Our Motherland

Give me one reason why Cameroon should crumble under the weight of debt, of political instability, mismanagement, and corruption. Are his children of inferior intellect? Are they inferior in dexterity? Can you see her mathematicians, philosophers, poets, artists, sportsmen and answer "yes"? Doesn't she have sons and daughters serving in top organizations, spearheading breakthroughs in space research, information technology, and strategic management? All that is needed is for her to wake up from her two decades or so of sleep, and take up her true rank in the hierarchy of nations. I call for a new nation to adopt the national ideals of service and progress. These ideals could very well be seen as deriving from our motto "Patrie" and "Travail." But I rather stress service and progress.

Since our ancestral times, our tribes have lived side by side till the advent of invaders. Some of us have proudly attempted to defend our independence; yet they were defeated with the help of our fellow countrymen. Under the guidance of the masters, we have acquired a pseudo-independence and achieved unification in 1972. Since our national ship has sailed, it has taken many to the shore of joy, happiness and self realization. But today, the ship seems to have sprung a leak; it got damaged by our own doing. Whatever exactly the cause is, it does not matter. The disease is here. The question is: what would you do? Would you go about quarreling among ourselves, casting blame on this tribe or that ethnic group? Or would you unite together and devote your best effort to plug the hole? Let us give our hearts, our blood to this; And if we fail in the attempt, let us sink with no curse on our lips for our fellow countrymen.

I advocate a return to our source, to our national soul. Where is it? One must ask. If our national soul can be worded, I would say it rests on the idea that every individual in the community must yield in their personal ambition to work for the success of the community as a whole. What is the use of keeping our soul in such a communitary value? Why not keep it in social or political independence? A social and political independence supposes the existence of greater love for one's country. But that seems not the case for now.

Maybe our national football team and its performance is the greatest metaphor for the return to the source. In that team, countrymen from various ethnic groups, countrymen from the mainland and the diaspora unite in love, in creative strategy, and in hard work to give our country its true place in the hierarchy of nations. In our national soccer team, the egos tend to disappear. Keep that spirit, educate our Youth among those channels, and we will have a stronger nation, a prosperous coun-try. Be aware of the cynical politician who will instrumentalize our national football team to blind you to your daily reality. Stay alert.

In every country, only a handful of powerful individuals dictate the fait accompli. The rest follow. I looked at our national assembly, our sen-ate, and our government. Now the question is: Who are these men of power in Cameroon? Those who are giants in sacrifice, who love their countrymen, and support their country. It is they who lead our society, and it is they again who change our social laws. When neces-sity demands it, we listen to them silently and do what they command.

First, try to understand this: does man make law or do laws make men? Does man make money or money make men? Does man make fame and name, or do name and fame make man? Be a man ; and you will see how your reality will be impacted. If you believe, you are born not as a tree, not a dog, not an ant , but a man. Please leave some mark behind you when you leave this planet.

Few nations have resisted the love and the sincerity of our national football team in the eighties and nineties. Marodonna's Argentina reckons with our sincerity and fearlessness. Then fear not even death. Brave lions, do not let the bark of puppies frighten you. Stand up, hold up and work.

Cameroon will be raised with the power of love, creative work, and dexterity; not with the flag of destruction, secession, oppression, repressive laws and policies, but with the flag of peace, of extensive freedom, and the rule of just laws.

Cameroon suffers from a great defect. We seem not to think of what we can pass on when are gone. We are fearful to take our ambition beyond the personal. We seem to see just the tip of our nose. We are short of leaders, short of people determined to move forward. They insist upon shouting from safe positions. How many Um Nyobes, Ernest Oundies, or Amadou Ahidjos? They are dead. But their ideals are not lost. In fact, our nation suffers because it has not yet reconciled with those ideals of independence such as self reliance. We continue to be ruled by puppets. Where is a Kagame? A leader who can masterfully enter into the chaos and steer his land toward success from the grip of the patriarchal relationships. Look at America and its high spirit of independence and its equal spirit of obedience to the highest ideals worded in its constitution. We are so self-important; we change the law to fit the whims of incompetent leaders. Hence no transformational work is produced in our nation.

The chief justice of Ghana once asked US supreme court Justice Stephen Breyer to explain to her how American people show such an obedience to the ruling of the Court. You see, perfect obedience to just law, perfect obedience to the highest ideals, are attitudes that lead to individual and national renaissance.

Jealousy, selfishness and the feeling of self-importance are to be banned from our national character. Young lions from our motherland, the whole work is upon your shoulders. You are destined to do this. No octagenerian can take you to the path of vigor, his legacy is behind him. Thank him for having neither helped nor seriously hurt our country; And take over. Put yourself to the task. Right now, more than ever, our country wants the spirit of brave warriors in the battlefield of life, not the idiots who look upon life only as a pleasure-garden!

My mission at this time is to arouse within you the ideal of warriors. I have entered myself into the journey of the warrior accompanied by tremendous music. So I am here to tell you that with no strength in the body, no enthusiasm in the heart, and no originality in the brain, we are just kilos of dead flesh! Bring life into them. Be fearless! Arise.

A handful of men can transform this country onto the right track, pro-vided they unite in thoughts, words, and actions. The more opposition there is, the better. But look! The fool is firing upon the opposition instead of wisely guiding it. Electricity was created because of the dam. The river continues fruitlessly rushing unless there is resistance. Look at advanced democracy, it involves the debates between opposing parties. It is the opposition which foretells the success. But in our motherland , the old lion , for the past twenty years and so, has either mustered or bought the opposition, instead of outsmarting the opposition with the people as a legitimate referee. Can you say our motherland is more successful today than it was thirty years ago?

Let us all work hard. This is no time to sleep. On our work depends the future of Cameroon. She is only sleeping. Arise, awake this motherland of ours.

Now you understand our sickness. With no more words of condemnation, close your lips and let your heart feel. Work out the salvation of this land, and that of neighboring countries. I agree with Professor Elikia Bokolo: Central Africa and Cameroon within, is the trigger of the gun called Africa. Work, work. Be servants while leaders. Be unselfish and waste less time in conferences. Let the true elites of each field of science organize conferences. Just work. Be industrious. Work as if the whole work of lifting our country depends on each of you.

What we want are young men and women willing to show abnegation and sacrifice for our country. We should first educate them, and then some real work can be expected.